To: _____

From: _____

Other books by Gregory E. Lang:

Why a Daughter Needs a Dad
Why a Son Needs a Dad
Why I Love Grandma
Why I Love Grandpa
Why a Son Needs a Mom
Why a Daughter Needs a Mom
Why I Chose You
Why I Love You
Why I Need You
Why We Are a Family
Love Signs

BROTHERS
AND SISTERS

100 Reasons Our
Relationship Is Like No Other

GREGORY E. LANG

CUMBERLAND HOUSE

NASHVILLE, TENNESSEE

Brothers and Sisters
Published by Cumberland House Publishing, Inc.
431 Harding Industrial Drive
Nashville, TN 37211

ISBN-13: 1-978-58182-511-4
ISBN-10: 1-58182-511-0
Cover design: Unlikely Suburban Design
Text design: Lisa Taylor
Photographs and cover photo: Gregory E. Lang

Printed in the United States of America
2 3 4 5 6 7 8 9 10— 11 10 09 08 07 06

To my siblings, David, Kevin, Jody, and Jennifer, and my children, Meagan and Linley.

INTRODUCTION

I began life as an only child. Thankfully, my parents had the foresight to give me a baby brother to assure that I would always have a ready playmate. When they saw how much I enjoyed him, they soon gave me two more. I always had a great time playing with my three younger brothers, climbing trees, digging holes in the backyard, collecting worms, and other such little boy stuff. But being the kind of child who wanted all life had to offer, I eventually asked them for a little sister. They happily gave me one of those, too.

Today, in my mid-forties, I cannot imagine my life without my brothers and sister. The five of us, just over seven years apart from the oldest to the youngest, have been comrades since day one. We did all the things happy siblings do together. We rode our bikes every day, spent weekend nights sleeping outside under the stars, celebrated each other's birthdays, taught one another how to do things, pushed each other around once in a while, fought about who got to sit by the window in the station wagon, played tricks on one another, tattled on one another, kept secrets for each other, and each night shared a home-cooked meal together at the same table with our parents.

We have at different times paired off in various combinations, depending on our ages and the life challenges facing us at the moment. Still, we always managed to come back together regularly as a unified bunch. In spite of the years that have passed since we all left the nest of our childhood home, we have not lost the special bond that ties us together. We know this to be true because every time we return to our parents' home and take our places on the front porch, laughter quickly erupts, teasing pours forth, occasionally a few happy tears flow, and we all linger there together as long as possible before rising to go our separate ways. And though we spend more time physically separated than together, we are always on one another's minds. I know this, too, because we call each other often between visits.

My family of four travels with me when I go to my hometown to visit my parents and siblings. My daughter and stepdaughter love to sit alongside me and witness these front-porch reunions. This is when they have the pleasure of hearing far too many embarrassing stories about me, when they get to see me in a different, less serious light, and when they get to see how close I am to my family. It is also when, I hope, they are taking note of what rich rewards await them as they continue to develop their own sibling relationship.

You see, my child was an only child, as was my stepdaughter, until I remarried a little over a year ago. Prior to our marriage, my then-fiancée and I independently regretted that our children had been denied the experience of growing up with a sibling. As we moved closer to marriage, one of the benefits we looked forward to was the combining of our small families, which would result in our girls becoming sisters. In the beginning, the new family was a bit of a challenge for both of them. They suddenly were required to negotiate, take turns, share, and compromise. Although my wife and I were troubled by these little conflicts, we knew it was a necessary and important process for the girls to go through. We shared the belief that siblings give one another a richer context for personal growth than can be had as an only child. We felt that by bringing them together through our marriage, we were better preparing them for their adult lives.

As we move forward in the second year of the formation of our new family, I see evidence that our daughters are indeed coming together as siblings. While each retains many of her previous "only child" personal habits, they have also formed new ones—"sisterly" ones. They advise each other on what to wear, share their shoes, shop and get their nails done together, negotiate their plans for the weekend so both get a little of what they want, keep each other's secrets, tattle on one another, laugh aloud as they make fun of the adults in the house, and stick up for each other to make sure neither is left out of anything we might do. Recently one said she looked forward to the day she would become an aunt, a role she thought not long ago she would never get to play.

My brothers and sister have given me a lifelong feeling of continuity. They ground me in a history that keeps me humble, belonging, and appreciative. They provide me with companionship I can always count on and enjoy. They make me laugh. They give me the kind of love that cannot be found elsewhere. More recently, they have been doing something for me they probably don't even recognize. They have embraced my new family with enthusiasm and treat my stepchild as if she has been their niece all along. They help me to create for both of these young girls an example of what wonders lie ahead for them as they move forward as sisters. For this, I thank them. For this, I love them even more.

The last photograph in this book, the one of five adults sitting on a columned porch, is of my siblings and me. The smiles on our faces are real; we were just teasing my two girls, who were trying to help me pose that photograph. As you can see, we still have a great time when we are together. We always will; it is our lasting commitment to one another.

BROTHERS AND SISTERS

BROTHERS AND SISTERS

can cheer one another up like no one else can.

BROTHERS AND SISTERS

give each other some of the best advice.

BROTHERS AND SISTERS

look up to and respect each other.

BROTHERS AND SISTERS . . .

can be counted on to keep a secret.

stand up for one another in times of doubt.

protect each other from harm.

know when to give each other a little time and space.

BROTHERS AND SISTERS

have a way of knowing what is on each other's mind.

BROTHERS AND SISTERS

make a house a fun place to live.

BROTHERS AND SISTERS . . .

do their best to keep one another from getting into trouble.

do things for one another without having to be asked.

won't allow one another to make major mistakes.

keep each other humble.

BROTHERS AND SISTERS

are the best present parents can give.

BROTHERS AND SISTERS

won't let distance keep them apart.

BROTHERS AND SISTERS . . .

never tire of telling each other, "I love you."

comfort each other when one is afraid.

do not shy away from each other's tears.

give each other tough love when necessary.

BROTHERS AND SISTERS

always try to be fair with one another.

BROTHERS AND SISTERS

understand each other in a way no one else can.

BROTHERS AND SISTERS

make a family last forever.

BROTHERS AND SISTERS

enjoy a little competition once in a while.

BROTHERS AND SISTERS

stick together like peanut butter and jelly.

BROTHERS AND SISTERS

are each other's most objective critic.

BROTHERS AND SISTERS . . .

learn some of life's most valuable lessons from each other.

always take each other's phone call, no matter
how late it might be.

plan together for how best to take care of their parents.

won't put up with less than should be expected of each other.

BROTHERS AND SISTERS

can communicate without using words.

BROTHERS AND SISTERS

share a love that always grows and never fades.

BROTHERS AND SISTERS

provide guidance for one another so that nobody becomes lost.

BROTHERS AND SISTERS

never fail to see the best in each other.

BROTHERS AND SISTERS . . .

have the best pillow fights.

like to wrestle in the grass.

know how far to take a joke without going too far.

never get too old to hug one another.

BROTHERS AND SISTERS

support each other in all of life's challenges.

BROTHERS AND SISTERS

make each other's life more fun!

BROTHERS AND SISTERS

are God's way of making sure a child is never lonely.

BROTHERS AND SISTERS . . .

understand one another's pain, but won't let
each other wallow in it.

seem to show up in each other's life at just the right time.

can see through each other's facade.

never need to warm up to each other; the love is always there.

BROTHERS AND SISTERS

can put a smile on each other's face in an instant.

BROTHERS AND SISTERS

are sensitive to each other's tender spots.

BROTHERS AND SISTERS . . .

don't just stand by and watch when one
of their own is down and out.

protect each other from monsters, bullies, and broken hearts.

need each other to better understand their parents.

need each other to better understand their homework.

BROTHERS AND SISTERS

never tire of each other's company.

BROTHERS AND SISTERS

can say things to one another that no one else can.

BROTHERS AND SISTERS

revel in each other's goofiness.

BROTHERS AND SISTERS . . .

become trusted uncles and aunts.

pass family traditions from generation to generation.

sacrifice for the benefit of one another.

can fill a treasure chest with wonderful memories.

BROTHERS AND SISTERS

look forward to seeing each other
after times of separation.

BROTHERS AND SISTERS

strive to overcome their differences.

BROTHERS AND SISTERS

can have fun doing nothing.

BROTHERS AND SISTERS

do not hesitate to show their affection for each other.

BROTHERS AND SISTERS

are always there for each other, without exception.

BROTHERS AND SISTERS

are each other's most loyal fan.

BROTHERS AND SISTERS . . .

take turns being the line leader.

always watch each other's back.

help each other with the chores.

teach each other how to do things.

BROTHERS AND SISTERS

may grow up but never grow apart.

BROTHERS AND SISTERS

forgive one another without having to be asked.

BROTHERS AND SISTERS

will not forget about one another, no matter what.

BROTHERS AND SISTERS . . .

can't help but make fun of each other once in a while.

conspire to keep their parents young.

can never stay mad at each other for very long.

aspire to be like one another.

BROTHERS AND SISTERS

share what they know to help each other learn.

BROTHERS AND SISTERS

can't help but get into a little mischief now and then.

BROTHERS AND SISTERS

understand each other's idiosyncrasies.

BROTHERS AND SISTERS . . .

encourage each other when the going gets tough.

do not betray each other.

will come to each other's rescue on a moment's notice.

never keep score or hold grudges.

BROTHERS AND SISTERS

help each other to look their best.

BROTHERS AND SISTERS . . .

let each other bask in the spotlight on birthdays.

know how to keep the party rocking!

know when to laugh and when to comfort.

lend a helping hand without expectation of reward.

BROTHERS AND SISTERS

are each other's cherished connection to the past.

BROTHERS AND SISTERS

can get on each other's nerves but always get over it.

BROTHERS AND SISTERS

share a bond that cannot be found anywhere else.

BROTHERS AND SISTERS . . .

won't let each other get away with things they
shouldn't get away with.

help each other remember what's important.

call each other now and then just to say hello.

love to tell those old, embarrassing stories over and over again!

BROTHERS AND SISTERS

know when to give each other a constructive push.

BROTHERS AND SISTERS . . .

offer each other a shoulder to lean on.

share with one another generously.

sometimes show their love in unique ways.

always include each other in the fun stuff.

BROTHERS AND SISTERS

watch over each other with love and affection.

BROTHERS AND SISTERS

are lifelong friends.

ACKNOWLEDGMENTS

Once more I owe a heartfelt thanks to Ron Pitkin, my publisher, who continues to have faith in the things I want to write about, and to the staff at Cumberland House, most notably my editor, Lisa Taylor, a trusted resource. I also thank my wonderful wife, Jill, for her unwavering support and faith in me, and our girls, Meagan and Linley, who keep our house a home. Finally, I thank my parents, Gene and Dianne Lang, for providing me the family they did.

TO CONTACT THE AUTHOR

write in care of the publisher:
Cumberland House Publishing
431 Harding Industrial Drive
Nashville, TN 37211

or e-mail the author:
greg.lang@mindspring.com